COSMIC TANTRUM

COSMIC TANTRUM

POEMS

SARAH LYN ROGERS

Curbstone Books / Northwestern University Press
Evanston, Illinois

Curbstone Books
Northwestern University Press
www.nupress.northwestern.edu

Printed in the United States of America

10 9 8 7 6 5 4 3 2 1

Library of Congress Cataloging-in-Publication Data

Names: Rogers, Sarah Lyn, author.
Title: Cosmic tantrum : poems / Sarah Lyn Rogers.
Other titles: Cosmic tantrum (Compilation)
Description: Evanston, Illinois : Curbstone Books/Northwestern University Press, 2025.
Identifiers: LCCN 2024056601 | ISBN 9780810147935 (paperback) | ISBN 9780810147942 (ebook)
Subjects: LCGFT: Poetry.
Classification: LCC PS3618.O467 C67 2025 | DDC 811/.6—dc23/eng/20241125
LC record available at https://lccn.loc.gov/2024056601

If in place of a mentor you had a hostile mirror. If you tested well. Were a pleasure to have. In class. In anywhere, under disapproval's burning kiss. If at recess you sat at the wall. Not in penance, but to trance out with markers—electric shades and planetary names. Each color intense, more itself against the others. (What could that mean.) If you gave future-you assignments. Tasks: they could never not love you back. Maybe you'd flip over the chin-up bars, your mind a quiet zoo. Maybe you could hear the trees, their secret names, pebbles begging for rides in your pockets. Listener, holder: I love you back. This is for you if you napped in the grass, unidentified object in an open field. If an adult woke you, gentle, said, I thought a child might be hurt. *If you're the adult. If time is a backhanded promise.*

let me stay tender-hearted, despite despite despite

—Chen Chen

CONTENTS

COSMIC TANTRUM

FATE MYTH WITH MANUFACTURED NEED

In a myth blamed on the stars, some woman
in a tower gave a gift you must repay.

Gift is euphemism. This is *debt.* You must
endeavor your whole life to free her. Loophole:

What if it doesn't take your whole life?
The townspeople just laugh. Each day you rise

to the occasion of demands. *Hurry! Now!*
Scale stones, plummet, shatter, reconstitute.

You don't look like you're climbing very hard.
The tower is the town's essential structure.

It casts its long, treacherous shadow.
Nobody knows who put her inside, or why.

There is only the wailing. Townspeople check
their sundial, give you a look like *This century,*

please. Their urgings boil your blood. You say
You do it, then, sacrilege against the myth.

They will not. If you free the woman-in-the-tower,
you think, then she's just some woman.

What would that do to a person.
You start to give less of a fuck.

One night you emerge from the trees
where you've wandered to clear your head

of hot coals. You catch her with a rope
ladder. She clings to it, patching mortar

between stones. Pleased with her work.
Your whole body ignites.

DESPITE MANY PROCLAMATIONS, LITTLE EDIE NEVER LEAVES BIG EDIE AT GREY GARDENS

I hate to spend the winter here. Oh, God,
another winter, Little Edie says
as the documentary concludes around her.

Mist and wind and the coming cold
descend on a woman who sees herself girl
and prisoner, posing near a hole

chewed by raccoons. Cute pests. She feeds them
Wonder bread, living for thanks, a kiss of spotlight.
Receives these when she worships at the feet

of a self-appointed god. Edie is the only supplicant,
mixed up about it. Of two minds, she has given her
whole life. *Any little mouse hole, any little rat hole . . .*

I would like better, she says, like a child,
huffy, stuffing a bindle for a film-ready escape—
the runaway makes it as far as the driveway

but turns back, into the charms of intimate chaos,
comfort of known discomfort. She's a tantrum:
flashy clothes, fifty years old and playacting adult

for rare visitors. Loneliness so palpable
the audience winces. She gives a mother something
to gloat over: See, there's nothing for you,

not out there.

GUIDED MEDITATION WITH MEAN VOICE

Oh, so we're doing this again.

Okay, breathe in, close your eyes,
you fucking loser, what makes
you think you deserve any time,

always behind in the mornings,

misplaced your keys, can't find
the shoes you wanted, O
enlightened being, that's rich.

The problem is you, the part
that covets self-destruction
despite your stated intentions—

isn't that right? Some defect,

admit it, desire for failure,
the reason your brain races
and you phone-scroll, aimless,

the reason your body doesn't want

to wake before noon, or fall asleep
before two. If you were good, couldn't
you handle all you were handed,

keep your home spotless clean,
call everyone who might be lonely?
Thicken your skin, practice old etiquette,

never need? Why can't you measure up

to what they want? (Give in,
give in, to this insistent
private hissing.)

WARM BLANKET TANTRUM

Young, I was sentenced "uninteresting,
but comfortable—like a warm blanket"
by a teenage boy who'd been *interested*,

all right, in a hole in my body. How long
can someone write about ambivalence
without the sadness hottening to anger.

How long can someone write about holes.
In a memory. Where other people have
their certainty. In someone else's story.

How could anyone love someone
made of holes. Discipline's exalted
in a hole. Inside, it hears the echo

of its voice, its only love. The boy asked
without asking what the world does
in so many words. When I say hole I mean

absence. When I say hole I mean void.
When I say void I mean the pity again,
a black hole. Discipline means punishment

or study. In this essay I will
nothing. I will vacant. Are you
comfortable yet. Are you warm.

BABY ISLAND

What is a daughter but a tiny mother
a book called BABY ISLAND seems to ask

without despair. I have never needed
to sniff a fresh neck. Never my hammock

of arm beckoning at a party. The girls
in the book are so young, ten and twelve.

They love babies and are useful—
what else does anybody need to know?

Oh yeah, the shipwreck. Their purses
full of sewing kits and chocolates.

Girls: they make the machine go.
On the island, they're in charge

of four helpless cherubs—paradise!
Rescued on Christmas Day—how marvelous!

Why do the stellar reviews make me cry
the way I do at catalogs of plastic grass

and Day-Glo eggs and truffles iced
with tenderness, and stuffed toys—

how from little ones they dangle like
loose teeth. The title of the book neglects

the girls, *so mature for their age*,
who dutifully dutied their duties

ten or twenty years ahead of schedule.
Why was labor the only adventure dreamt for them.

ELDEST DAUGHTER TIME TRAVELS, BODY SWAPS THROUGH GLITCH IN MATRIX; WELCOME LOCAL BEAST

To lap at the sweet nectar
of a punctured Stretch Armstrong

I wear a beinghood
less mutable. Now *I* am

the secondborn, a magic trick-
ster. *Now you see me,*

too spirited. An only child
if born first, they report

as though being beastlike
voids the contract

of existence—*poof!*
No more tantrums

over toppled cup-stacks,
ruined homes of cards!

My audience vacillates
through wrath, often rapt.

I raise the blanket to the air
and disappear.

WHAT IS THE BIRD IN CHARLIE BROWN'S NAME?

sympathy for Charlie, a mere child
who understandably stress-lost
all his hair

in his world a voice of reason
is a plunger-muted trumpet

and trust as a choice knocks him
flat on his back, every time

HA HA HA HA

what is the bird in Charlie Brown's name
someone asks, taking liberties
with syntax

they want "Woodstock"
but have blown this thing wide open

little creature
hiding in the phonemes

I know you now
a counterweight
to AAUGH

only Charlie sees you
in his third eye

when they sound him
like complaint

GENRE STUDY

Grey Gardens is a fairy tale run backward.
Now it's a ghost story. Gone, handsome princes.

Gone, king of the estate. The mansion crumbled
into the idea of a place. These women: haunted

by the life they ruled as debutantes, most eligible
face. Gone, that social standing. Gone, their currencies

of youth and beauty. Big Edie spent hers on a man
who had real money. He spent her and left her

alone in that house. Little Edie spent some
of herself on suitors, the rest on her mother.

Now they make of each other a world. Child-parent,
future-past, hero-antagonist, jailer-savior, hope-fear:

all things to all (two) people. They're all they have,
grateful and pissed. Each woman sees in the other

her mirror. Or the well they've fallen down,
cannot allow each other to climb from. Now

it's a tragedy. The house, still nice, was too dear
to convert to currency. Maybe it felt like a fortress

against shame. No such thing. No matter how grand
the façade. Time-lapse. Look: decrepit, valueless asset.

Holes in the roof. The external world creeps in.
Come, forest critters. Come, errand boy and cameras.

Through decades, through desiccated vines and thorns.
Through a twisted version of a home. Inside, you'll find

no spinning wheel, queen mother, or princess to awaken
with a kiss. Just two people resigned to stay asleep in this.

VERMIN

A roach corpse is stuck by its legs in adhesive
on the laundry room floor of the new New York
apartment, reminding me of Kafka's hapless hero

and how a shadow part of me felt envy
for the ghost of his accountability
vanishing with his human body,

how he kissed his salesman life goodbye
once changed *into a monstrous vermin*
like the old-Europe folk costumes

in which I someday hope to dance—
eight feet tall, long-necked in goatskin
or with an alligator's craggy mouth

and cartoon eyes—all huge, anonymous
monsters not held responsible
for anybody's happiness.

I fear change, but I fear stagnation
more. *Is this all?* is enough
to make me unstick my legs.

Someone who says they love me
will not visit—perhaps afraid to ride
the trains, to feel impotent and small

the way I've always been, this skin
I wear. Now I resist the pull to vanish;
I assume the guise of beasts. The stuck

roach corpse's horror is inertia: dying
knowing what you need to live
needs you to move.

UNIVERSALLY RELATABLE WRITING PROMPTS, PART I

Write about school assignments that asked you to recall specific life experiences. (And how, years later, speakers hired by your employer would ask the same, for team building.) Write about presumptions of universality. As though everyone alive has, by a certain age, certain memories.

Write what you learned over summer vacation.

Write about a time you defended a friend from a bully.

Write about a barely coherent explosive argument whose subtext made sense only decades later.

Write about a summer vacation from your youth when a blood relative asked you to enter a wet T-shirt contest.

Write about living through a framework where cause and effect makes no sense, as though a mouse spontaneously generates from trash.

Write about fairy tales, where good-enough mothers are offed early. A daughter (always a daughter) is left with her wits and the fawn response. In fairy tales, people sell (out) their daughters. They'll trade away her labor, her firstborn, her severed hands, her life. To a creditor. For clout. To save face. To atone for a crime. A kept daughter creeps along the floorboards, or aloft, entombed in the air. Always the threat of the woods (of other people). The parents/stepparents agree on nothing but its treachery, describe her as a sitting duck, a pie cooling in an open window. The woods are full of threats and she's a fool. The woods are full of thieves and she's a purse.

Write about tying your shoes together at age seven to see if, like in cartoons, you'd fall flat on your ass. Hmm. Write about carrying them to the principal's office, barefoot, because nobody, not even your teacher, could untie them.

Write about what fiction workshop feedback reveals about people. For instance: "I don't understand why this woman can't just decide what she wants and then do that."

Write about the word *admit*, which used to mean *allow*. How now it means *confess*. Admit one.

Write about finding a twelve-thousand-word blog post on the "real reason" Big and Little Edie were *like that*. Write about why it's easier to believe two women went insane from toxic mold than from each other. The writer gives as evidence that Little Edie's brain function improved once she lived in a well-ventilated place by the ocean. Write about how, also, she lived alone, in a place of her choosing, near other people.

Write about a lineage of ghosts. A house haunted by the living.

Write about your emotional response to first seeing the Babugeri, three figures with uncanny silhouettes, furred necks stretched plantlike toward the sun—these beings against meadow and mist, looking like they crept into the photo from your subconscious. In their strangeness, an unyielding beauty. Write about the humans in those monster costumes, cradled there, in ritual play.

Write about the times kids invited you home for playdates and then wouldn't let you leave.

Write about being young and old. Think Childlike Empress. Little Edie Bouvier. Harold's Maude. Charlie Brown. A three-thousand-year-old elf with Liv Tyler's face. A baby crone. A new stone. New water.

Write about having weak gravity. How easily you're sucked into orbit.

Write about your early fear of transforming into *a brat*, the worst monster. Write about being summoned to pass exhausting litanies of tests, to prove that you were no beast but a real girl, a good one (and who gets to determine this). Write about this as a default template for relating.

Write about your reaction to an attachment-trauma patient calling other people *the humans*.

Write about Big Edie telling her daughter *The only vermin here is you*.

Write against the idea of people as DIY projects. Write about this question: "If this person stays exactly as they are now for the rest of our lives, do I still want to be this close to them?" Write about people who've wanted you, desperately, but not this you.

Write about a dogmatic corporate environment's effects on an already-tenuous sense of self.

Write about powering a small electrical grid with the intensity of your emotions.

Write about your second-grade vitriol for Ramona Quimby, a child who couldn't get her shit together.

APPLICANT MUST HAVE

somewhere to live, like anyone
who'd prefer
self-determination to a
curse in ancestral line
or a door that opens only to reveal
the secret
horrifying will and
STEM education
what's an approvable
pile of gold
kid
cat
remaining wish?
someone of consequence
—a signature
in exchange for this
vital thing, six walls
a lot

with a salary forty times monthly rent,
fifty billion in savings, or
shit-eating grin
kept in check by side hustle,
SO many bank statements and
handshake of the Freemasons, a
testament to a submission kink
AND/OR starter wife—
desperation
AND one (1) weak point in armor?
OR one (1) cat but not both?
OR one (1) dog but not both?
on a monkey's paw: *to have been*
not overpowered, not revealed
the true name to vanquish applicant
one tiny
pixel of land
of fucking nerve

RENTER

Each dusk, the ravens who know no borders
bed down within the country club. I have seen this
from hilltops and through holes in a tall fence,
spying what I haven't been shown, like a past

I know only obliquely—in a household's two sets
of silverware, "one from my first marriage,"
an utterance conveying a life story no one
really told me, though I glimpsed it

in a forty-year-old photo of a stranger:
him youthful and tan, his widow-to-be
beaming the way the young do
before the wattage gets snuffed. Not yet

extinguished. Looking, I felt I had leapt
a tall fence, staring in at what another owns,
the way I once glanced through my neighbors'
curtainless front window at their grand piano,

their Christmas tree still stately and enormous
the first week of March, which is when I got caught
peeking. The woman at her tree narrowed her eyes
at me, embarrassed on the sidewalk. *How dare you*

look her look said, when what I'd seen wasn't hidden.
I know that nothing on this earth is mine, that everything
I think I own is leased. The ravens know it, too.
The woman in the photo learns too soon.

HALLOWEEN AND I'M THE ONLY ONE IN COSTUME ON THE SUBWAY

today I am willfully unbeautiful
and really freaking out
this guy holding
the subway pole with me

behold the animal fear in him
when my voice escapes
a mismatch borrowed form

and at the office
such stiff, scared grins

I have never been so frightening
not since I cut my princess hair
into a pompadour

today I crown myself
lord of minor misrule
and no one utters *Sarah.*

(Did you feel me
            reinhabit
                        that small form?

What if I
            were eight feet tall,
                        obscured by goat hide?
                                    Or a sentient bundle of reeds?

This is a power

            I had
                        never before
                                    seized.)

SUBTWEETED AGAIN IN THE SHARED GOOGLE DOC

I hacked in like the best
shouting *access the mouse*
yelling *enhance* at rectangles
in my cybercrime uniform

I'm in

black longsleeve and a ski mask
Shutterstock portrait of a predator
decoding your contempt
which could be strengthened
with at least one special character

my gloved hand portals the screen
I unzip files
exposing a familiar code
the wicked pleasure of feeling wronged

who, knowing it would unmake them,
could believe in tenderness?

if everyone else is a whetstone
then you always know yourself
to be the knife

NOT EVERYONE WOULD SOONER KILL YOU THAN ADMIT YOU HURT THEIR FEELINGS

trumped, the aspiring dictator plays
an invisible concertina

in the puffed-up way of a snake
who has swallowed a lightbulb

I have seen that X-ray
favored curio of my grandfather

in his office trove of news clippings
cloistered there for anecdotes

on hallucinogenic crisis
the disbelieved wound

of the projector screen—dalí
and van gogh were both named

for their dead brothers
my grandfather too

a real boy in the void
shaped by a ghost

his stories polished stones
wrapped like hard candies

self-contained, untouchable
sustenance-myth of the unwanted

now I call myself a real girl
seething at the narcissist in chief

who's fluent in complaint
my mother tongue

and who asserts existence through contagion—
rotten orange spreads its mold

to the others in the bowl: *now you*
are also me, therefore I am

threatening civil war is sport to him
only one of these men feels

how to obliterate another
is a violence

I COULD SIGNAL DOMINANCE IN EMAIL CORRESPONDENCE AS TRAINED BUT THE CONCEPT IS OFFENSIVE AND I'M BABY

To retain your power,
drop the "I," said somebody

dead, whose wife probably
typed his manuscripts. She might

have been a tree, a shooting star,
otherworldly spirit in a housedress,

maybe was. We'll never know—
nobody took dictation for her shit.

So w(e)ary of the phrase "the industry."
I, I, I, I, the angel speaks herself,

in a gay fantasia on national themes,
her light dimmed that it might be visible

to lesser "I"s. Don't tell me not to be
an "I." Be what, somehow-imposing

conduit for info passed direct
to consumer? I, I, I, I am not.

There is only one "I" in "sin-eater."
And only one wrong way to eat a Reese's

(NSFW). Slogan, "I"less dialect
of business; the boys' club learns withholding

(their “I”s, much information) between power
stances at some seminar. With each dropped “I,”

the glass coffin ascends, unburdened
of a viewpoint. Sacred invocations

for the ages: “OK.” “confirm receipt.”
“under review.” “not at this time.”

LOCAL BEAST RECENTLY INHABITED SHARED SPACE

you may know her
by the usual signs

ghosts of ritual smoke

in the rooms pinched faces
have owningly tongued

clean, bare surfaces

beneath shower water
slick grace in an animal howl

how even the suggestion
of her presence ignites

your inner middle manager

little man loading his coins
into his automatic weapon

HALLOWEEN: "WHAT EVEN *ARE* YOU, ANYWAY?"

today no one whose money
earns their personhood

orders me
onto my knees

to blot their coffee
from the carpet

today I am not fit to parade
little trays to big guests

not in broadshoulder bulk
and secondhand clothes

really fucking up
the front-desk first impression

still, I answer phones, buy time,
pack-mule their wood and glass

under nylon wig and beard
in this borrowed body, the usual

eyesore, footman, bumpkin
pillow-padded, sweaty

today I chose to embody the joke
dressed as my archetype, the admin

from that middle-grade series
that must not be named

the wild man—the bear—
okay, the groundskeeper

serving the powerful
who daren't stoop

NO ONE WANTS TO VOLUNTEER FOR AN EMBODIMENT ON EARTH ANYMORE

The guys up top entice us here with sweetness: raspberry hats supped
from a thumb, summer afloat belly-up in the sea, music in the chest's
clench and relief. *Bet you'd like to have a body*, they say. *Yours if you commit*

to these dimensions and fine print. Drawing breath, you consent to toil daily
in abstraction for an arbitrary chain of time, for years, to be allowed
to have a home and, in it, eat of food. Too much of this world's currency

is shame. Daily it accrues interest. Some are interested, all right.
But do not like your tone—aren't you aware that they are Good?
If they might not be Good, they might not *be*. Are you saying that you wish

that they were dead? (It sure sounds like you, a Bad, said that.)
Someone mouthing a soundbite to NEVer owe ANyone ANything
forgot or never got to be a child, renter, indentured therapist, fast-paced

self-starter whose talents include rumination, champagne taste on a Kool-Aid
budget, and squeezing blood from a rhinestone. The union rep says the real job
is to poke at every carefully laid fear, what the stranglers say you owe

for the discomfort of their hands. I have volunteered for earthside many times,
often to sate a sweet tooth, to be moved ugly to tears by sorrowed songs.
Each alternate reality (game) an amnesia. There are things you don't forget.

How punishment cannot
purchase affection.

Which kinds of wisdom
cost which kinds of grief.

Who gets to be a Good
and who a service.

A TOAST TO THE DISMAY OF CERTAIN INDUSTRIES

Each slice of toast a manicured lawn, green as savings,
the neon envy of bootstraps—long known for the raising
of boots and not the booted. A rumor spread by boots:

that upon their approach you play dead. No, get as big
as you can. Wave your arms. They're more afraid of you
than you of them. Ten fewer avocados till autonomy.

And then what should we do with these damn trophies?
First we award participation. To the diamond industry,
which should have shown up unannounced, with a résumé,

to indicate strong interest at our office of maligned
demographic affairs. To the napkin industry,
which honestly could have shown better initiative.

Inflated houses, we reject you first. Never bought us coffee,
nor saved your summer earnings for a whole year
of tuition, so go the legends from the luckiest

in human history, born and breaded on postwar production
abundance and unevenly allocated ease. Economists
with dowsing rods and dicks up for the market sure soften

with declining demand. Mark it, how they speak of loyalty,
invoke obedience expected to one's family. In the good
old days, this valley was all job orchards, for miles.

You could scrape your wrist across your fence and pull,
your kindly neighbor none the wiser. They don't make 'em
like that anymore. So pluckable, firm in the hand.

ARTFULLY VAGUE TRANCE

if you stay very general
you will always be right

many people have said this
smart people, Good people

the only ones you can trust
who know everything THEY

won't tell you—the simple truth
honest facts, the real scoop

we delight to inform you
about the latest threat

how it threatens you personally
and will harm your particular life

in ways we will outline shortly
after this commercial break

PLEASE ANSWER TO THE BEST OF YOUR ABILITY

where does your spirit hurt

do parts of yourself
feel missing or broken

can you resist the delicious call
of the ocean

when did you stop dancing

can you feel within yourself
that little girl who held, triumphant
a flaming skull

do you frequently wish you were dead
or think about ways to end your life

if you don't have a daily meditation practice
what's stopping you

why are you so resistant to yoga

would you describe this experience
as a dark night of the soul

have you tried not thinking about it

do you feel like a skeleton
whose flesh can only be revived
by a particular ancient song

how long have you experienced these symptoms

have you considered that the energy you put out
is what's coming back to you

don't you think you might be overreacting

why are you doing this to me

YOU ARE INSTRUCTED NOT TO ASK WHAT IT IS

You might say, "Tell me about this."
And there are clues: what's biggest in the frame,

how many fingers. For some reason the sky
won't touch the ground. That's fine—don't worry

over details like that. Worry over your own self,
skin and hair, this form that won't conform

or be obscured. Have your edges ever felt
so distended? In childhood you were—like any of us—

geometric, book of unlined paper, no marks.
Adults wore their experience like Scotch tape

dragged across the carpet. They picked up lint
and flecks, mysterious bumps. Things you felt

you oughtn't be able to see. Someone started it:
Experienced equated with *obscene*. How a folded page

can never unknow the line. How the mouth's assembly line
uproots the teeth you can't repot. You can't go back,

but you must go. Some days you feel like a raw hunk of meat,
set with wire and electrified—some unseen hand

pushes a button, makes you twitch. Some days a piano
squashes you cartoon-flat. You spit keys. Cannot

blow out your candles. Some days are deep-sea dives,
gathering specimens to understand. To understand what?

The answer.
In your mind, you build construction sites. You drive

one of the frightening machines. Here, you can lift
impossible weights. Break down and discard.

Nothing too much. Back to skin, looped image of a face
someone would give you: lip curl of yuck, ugly sneer.

(An expression for lint, loosed teeth, an errant pube.)
Why would somebody so often hand you this?

This wordless alphabet of disgust? With a child's pride,
as though passing a craft into your hands:

I made this. I made it for you.

GOLDEN CHILD TANTRUM

baby tired

as foretold in legend

baby hungry

as writ in the ancient tomes

baby gal pal

on white steed, wielding sword

baby give counsel

preordained keeper of secrets

baby take dictation

O, look thou: cherub fingers on th' keyboard

baby triangulate

verily she violates doctor-patient confidentiality

baby not real doctor

poor lady, she had better love a dream

baby doll

magic feather, amulet, rabbit's foot

baby mirror

yea, though some hath sworn she were a window

baby spin straw into gold

the fate of the miller's one beautiful daughter

baby finance microloan

a necklace, a ring, a firstborn to bequeath

baby invoke loophole

that to name the true name can unmake anything

baby mobilize resource

the unguessable name in her mouth, a sad grin

baby mean

the bested-one's fury splits him into two

baby old

how could splitting be the end of anyone

baby everything

and nothing

baby want

UNIVERSALLY RELATABLE WRITING PROMPTS, PART II

Write about the thousands of occasions in which someone wanted something from you, told you nothing about it, then became sullen and resentful because you hadn't yet given it to them. Parent, partner, roommate, boss—whoever. You're supposed to just know, or guess, and to provide. This is a baby's expectation of its primary caregiver. It's their expectation of you.

Write about an adult who used you as their nervous system.

Write about your emotional response to first reading "Innocence is a relic of a time when women had the same legal status as children. Innocence is beneficial to your owner. It benefits you not at all."

Write about how everyone believes they have good motives.

Write about endless petitions for proof. Prove you're too sick for school. For work. You don't look sick. Prove your income. Prove your point. Prove your innocence. Prove you have good motives. Prove it was that bad. Prove it wasn't. Prove you didn't mean it. Show your doctor's note. Your tax return. Your pay stubs and a letter from your employer. Do you deserve a raise. A home. Prove it.

Write about all the times being a Very Good, compliant, useful child / employee / tenant did not protect you from getting kicked to the curb.

Write about having a little self-respect, as a treat.

Write about how sometimes *innocence*'s opposite is *guilt*, and sometimes it's *experience*.

Write about someone who can't conceive of you being the main character in your own story because you're the sidekick in theirs. They cannot imagine you at the center of anything. You're either their sidekick, or someone else's.

Write about selling your hair.

Write about which is Charlie Brown's mask—the child self, or the adult self? Which is Little Edie's?

Write about how "You should want to" is a curse.

Write about the slow, infinite relay race of emails back and forth, back and forth, your ancestors peering down like *what the fuck*.

Write about the school principal, in one of your grandfather's many life-lesson anecdotes, who threatened, *I'm gonna break your spirit.* Actually said the words.

Write about whether yours are the socially sanctioned addictions or the ones favored by cautionary movie montages, ones people can see.

Write about how the phrase "It's just good business" is wielded like an incantation that can nullify wrongdoing.

Write about Norse and Greek myths, how they get it right, the gods fallible assholes like anyone.

Write about the moment after the flag dance when Little Edie says the only thing she needed *was this man!* and it feels camp, but it's so true? She was raised to need a man to win her and provide for her; that was to be her career. She needs this cameraman, needs another person's gaze, their emotional and material resources, needs the money from this film. She needs dialogue with more than one person, more than the only one she has.

Write about why nothing is so painful as receiving someone's warm generosity.

Write about a time someone you loved said, "Don't look now but those people over there just looked you up and down and made faces at each other like *Ew, how ugly.*"

Write about wondering why a soul would choose to incarnate here, but loving when a poem *devastates* you.

Write about how when a business advertises "We're like family," they mean a family run like a business. You could be some institution's Golden Child of the Month for the rest of your life and never win anything.

TANTRUM ABOUT MY UTERUS

how does one handle
being the bag
holding the prize
they want to touch

I want not to be squashed
like an overripe pumpkin
pushed by a stranger's
presumptuous palm

when my body becomes portal
I want for sanctuary a cave
and, standing sentry, wolves

and
to be the cave

and be the wolves

CROSS-SECTION OF THE NERVOUS/ SOLAR SYSTEM

though the map
is not the territory—

how we represent ourselves
to ourselves—to get to the heart
of what's the matter

look to the body at rest, supine, immovable
around which other bodies swerve and arc

a minor planet veering out of orbit
embeds itself in tiled floor again

towel pressed into the gap
below a closed door

broken capillaries
on the orbital

the Big Bang
is also

an origin
myth

SOME BRAINWASHED DUDE ON TWITTER INSISTS THAT TO BE VALUABLE A WOMAN MUST POSSESS THE MATHEMATICALLY PERFECT, SUSPICIOUSLY BABYLIKE SKULL OF AN ANGEL

and I'm like, Really, you mean a terrifying vortex
of uncountable wings and eyes
moving at incomprehensible speed,
so stabbing-bright that you are sore afraid?

and he text-sneers that No one wants
a hag, shifting the spotlight of shame
off himself, loving how it feels to aim it

at the heads of angular women, hard, barbed
beings of stone. He wants to inflate a pink bubble
with gas, his *film* opinions, how to ride a bike.

I'm like, That's only the most ancient of moves, dude.
Stone doesn't shrink at *ugly*. Is more than a hole
someone hopes to stuff. Knows fear by many faces

and how language spotlight-wielded
guises lack. You can't leach the sex appeal
from "witch skull," head of a woman
the limp declare too sharp.

TO MY TEENAGE SELF, WHO ALWAYS FELL FOR IT

Mostly I remember the phone calls.
I still see you in that red car, sweating with no air.
You knew *What do you think?* was a cage.

That summer, he won a single lovebird,
carried it behind bars to the yard, a lesser god.
You thought this was love: Someone holds you

in hot light. They make you sweat. You earn
your passing grade for half a day, your radius
cage-small. You prove you can live on so little.

The bird died. He left it too long in the sun.
You didn't know it then, but eventually,
you'd run.

GUIDED MEDITATION WITH INNER CHILD

She's you, but small, little sprout
ponytail, bare feet, crooked grin
scoopable, mischievous. One eye

closes slightly on one side
smiling bigger than the other. You
would never say harsh words

to her, never push her to exhaustion
or starvation, never sacrifice her
to save face. She gets restless

she needs soil, she needs time
alone to finger-paint or
photosynthesize. She needs water,

a nap, an afternoon snack.
She wants to be a tree,
concoct a potion, throw ashes

in the air, big blasts of smoke.
She needs to cry sometimes
and chase the cats. She needs

to know there's nothing she should prove—
no formula that means now she's
allowed. Hold her and feel held.

LITTLE EDIE'S VISIONS AND HER FLAG DANCE

Baby's first tap shoes
in a trash can —

bopped wrist, pinched ear —

"you can have them back
when you're older" —

parade float majorette —

soft-focus senior portrait —

Schrödinger's fiancée —

fallen leaf of the last tuft
of hair —

her pale skull
solemnly anointed
with Lycra —

how golden
she still is,
or could be.

Can they see this
Edie wonders
in my dance?

Certainly
the cameramen must

how her white pumps
raise the ghosts
of could have been —

her arm's decisive slicing
with the flag
some kind of sign — ?

Inside that crumbling mansion in the Hamptons
a remote
and unmoved eye.

THE CONTENT IS SUPPOSED TO BURST FROM THE CONTAINER

I cover the void with crystals
piling over it with amethysts and jasper.

In the center, not a pit but a dark mirror.
Scry in it and find your face.

I cover the void with bones.
Some kind of person

must feel a way about them.
Bones are not-void. Bones suggest

beinghood. Had-once-been-hood.
I cover the void in Bésame lipstick

the good shit, in tiny gold tubes.
Could a void give you a name brand?

Probably. I cover the void
with cinched waists, shoulder pads.

Nightly I embalm the void.
If nothing else, it will be succulent.

I cover the void with tarot cards
which are also emissaries to the void.

They return with dark mirrors.
To know the void is to know

almost nothing. I cover it
and nobody can see

what they can't see
they're not seeing.

LET'S PRACTICE KISSING, COMPARE BRA SIZES

The women, they are ripping off their skirts,
revealing shorter skirts, igniting
pyrotechnics in their wake.

The women wash their faces in slow motion,
floating water liquid crystal, that *deep clean*
money shot.

The women remember sleepovers, feeling
up friends with manicured hands, pillow fights
in underwear

backs arched and asses angled toward
their audience—*alone*, wink wink,
with the omnipresent gaze.

How in command they're made to look,
placed doll-like before fire, flood,
confetti of feathers.

When the women cry, faces smooth
as mirrors, their mascara
doesn't even run.

SHUT-IN TANTRUM

Itching when: I read Austen; at the aquarium,
I meet an eighty-year-old lungfish;
and, in disbelief, I watch *Grey Gardens.*

In *Sense and Sensibility*, Marianne practices
pianoforte scales, Elinor her sewing or whatever.
We watch them stave off boredom,

waiting for men to choose them. For anything
to happen. Why don't these shut-in women
jump through windows? Set things aflame?

Why doesn't Little Edie—real-life woman
confined to a dark, trashed mansion? She
and her mother float through the murk

of their tank, aware of their audience
and not, as we watch with popcorn
from the infinite, escapable side of the glass.

LOCAL BEAST WITHSTANDS RECORD-BREAKING SILENT TREATMENT

A beast pushed to the hedgerow
feels the pull of rampage

egged on by the scent
of weaponized silence.

When you know, you know
the stranglehold of someone

spoiled on Good, babied
by an enabler—sorry,

the *essential*
worthless tool

for granting
hinted wishes.

The beast has extra senses—
shape-shifts, flattens as small

as claimed space disallows,
smells every silent tantrum.

And the living room's
one never-ending fart.

And the kitchen is
one never-ending fart.

And the office is
one never-ending fart.

EGG TRANCE

have you ever cracked open an egg
and had a bunny rabbit fall out?
have you ever cracked open an egg
and had someone yell *shut the door*?

have you ever cracked open an egg
and used your thumb to smooth
it closed, hollow and whole?
have you ever done that to yourself?

have you ever poked a hole in an egg
at each end and blown the liquid goo
into a waiting bowl?
did you paint the egg? did you waste

the part that was not of interest?
when it was empty did you fill it
again—a whispered message?
did you then set it adrift on a stream?

or smash it under a hammer?

POT-BOUND

All winter, men are yelling in the walls.
The gas is out. Somebody smelled a leak.
The ghosts of cigarettes waft stories high.
This is how the year begins, already wrong.
Was it in my stars that I would never think
of *now*, that I would wall myself inside
of looping thoughts?

My brother lives here for only one season,
flown back to his home coast at the onset
of the plague. Don't think I will forget
how we cloister us indoors to hibernate
exactly when the daffodils burst through
their winter confinements, heralding . . .
what, exactly?

The men are gone. The scaffolding remains,
keeping my seedling body from the sun.
Some other season I'll emerge—blinking,
splitting off the husk of one who watched,
who waited—and maybe will believe in *now*,
then. Later.

"THAT'S ALL I NEED—AN ORDERED LIFE"

sympathy for Edie, a woman-child
who understandably stress-lost
all her hair

in her world a voice of reason
proves elusive—the dream house
is dark, occults its atmospheric pressures
and the centers of its storms

to the lightning rods, dowsers,
and weather vanes, initiates
into a par-tic-u-lar illogic

we see you
as she sees her horoscope

through a too-close
magnifying glass

SELF-ANTHROPOLOGY

to translate the emotions into images—

vestigial remnants, a procession of ghouls
watching the ancient statue start to crumble—

you take a bath in an old house
you cross a boundary and [X] happens

there's the story you tell yourself to endure an experience
and the story you must translate for others

who is conditional love's model pupil
why do you have no preferences

someone else's world is a desolate planet
people have starved on more

that clench of dread

there are feelings beyond logic
unpinnable by human tongue

still you know

Write about the Cinderellas. How, in one book, obedience is a curse. She can be ordered to love someone. To make stitches so small they are invisible. (The commands so small they are invisible; they feel like her actual desires.) No man can save her from this. But like the magic bag that grows to accommodate whatever's put in it, the smallness of her will learns to stretch.

In the animated film, her allies are animals. Her human family makes her feel worthless. They need her near so they can push her away and reel her back, resented and craved, craved and resented. You start to see it: they wouldn't smash her flat if they weren't afraid of her power. But in the end, her most important asset is her beauty, which carries her into a better life. This is supposed to be satisfying, this *Who, me?* revenge. What does she even say to this man, a stranger who wanted her because she left?

In a folktale, she is not called Cinderella but she lives the first half of Cinderella's life: dead father, new mother, ordered onto the floorboards. There is no man. She is pushed into the woods in search of fire. (Her light went out: the hearth, the heartbeat of the house, it's dead. The stones are cold. Everyone depends on her.) The keeper of the fire is an old, old woman who ran out of fucks hundreds of years ago. *You want fire? Separate these black specks from these other black specks*. Tasks like that. The ancestors watch over and the girl who is not Cinderella performs impossible feats. The old woman shrugs like *What do you want me to do, throw a party?* But she holds to her promise. *I keep my extra fire in this skull, for some reason. Carry it home*. The girl returns with the light, with knowledge of the wider world. The skull lights a fire, all right. It burns everything but her.

THE TOWNSFOLK ENACT A STRONGLY WORDED LETTER

Unwelcome beast! Why come you not when called?
Cloaked and torchlit at the hedgerow, we shout
that you might offer a response. We petition you, beast:

Unbeast yourself. You will hear our accusations:
Beast, you have hinted at anger. Harbored
unworshipful thoughts. Beast, you have loomed,

unmoving, at crossroads. Have accepted material gifts
but behaved as though not beholden. In short,
you have appeared as what you are. Do you deny it?

What would you pay to right this? We have the land
and title. You, these dubious woods they call
the commons. Come, beast. Unmuzzle your intent,

that shapeless animal galloping. Let us see
the fullness of its form, that we might stone it down,
cloven thing that cleaves the known we know.

Once was, you wanted to want what you were wanted
to want. Is there a simpler joy than this: a warm,
calm body in the room, felt presence, nothing more?

(Here our demands diverge: *Nothing* and *More*.)

AUTOCORRECT SUGGESTS “TITHE”

what want means
what the words even are
how to human
why void
where hearth
what teeth
who the asker
who that answers
why write it
when cavern
when mirror
who in cartesian theater
who running the projector
how to survive the feeling
that you won’t survive this feeling

THE EMPRESS

she needs a man who knows his anima
who can say what he needs or nothing
who can bow to the beast in her,
mistress of blood, refuse, and rage

who sees her like the pomegranate—
smooth, round, and rosy housing
many jagged facets, tumbled into
jewels in her belly as they scratch her

who knows this outer softness is hard-
won, the art of mothering without
feeling mothered, the art of holding
scars where no one can see them

except when she howls
and when she does he knows
not to balk or bark back

he knows what she said
of a dog's enduring love
was not about the dog

SYMPTOMS DEPEND UPON METHOD AND DURATION OF EXPOSURE

What else can I say about the girl-woman
who knows a love mercurial as the flag
on the end of her twirling baton?

She drinks it like the ancients did,
for immortality, the fantasy
of a personhood so powerful

it cannot be snuffed
by anyone, not by time,
not by death herself.

Or like the hatters
boiling felt
in poisoned vapor—

how they must have been mad
even before, or how could they
have done this every day?

IT'S THE LOCAL BEAST, CHARLIE BROWN

we need a win, Charlie
a chance to raise our noses

twelve o'clock
and dance the pony

something to show we're more
than bags of rocks

from smug adults
meant to teach us what, exactly

what's wrong with creature comforts
warm blue blanket, jazz piano

belief that superstitious wait
will be rewarded

for no reason other than
we asked, and seemed sincere

BEHOLD! she rises
wreathed in burrs and felines

stage-whispering—good grief!

I am the creature
comfort me

RAGE PRACTICE

When small, she'd lock her legs
against the force of it, unutterable
scream heat sucking the knees backward,

body knocked flat. She learned to pull
the impulse underneath. Ages pass.
Now the placid one loves night,

her only kingdom. She is recognized,
but not as what she is. Then the axe,
the wicker chair, the invitation.

Mimed violence opens space in a stuck
channel. The chopping gesture siphons
lava up: volcano, passing all these years

as mountain. And she is not a her she knows—
or now she is. All that is left of the wicker
is splinters. And there it is, strange ecstasy

like when that jawbone floated to her feet,
returned after the ocean heard her wish,
or when the wolf skull beckoned to be lifted

from its nest of leaves: *Ah, there you are / Here I am.*
A prescribed regimen of this. Practice—as in
meditation. Practice—as in something to perfect.

LOCAL BEAST KIND OF A LITTLE BITCH, ACTUALLY

in the game of psychic supplicant
nobody ever wins

the little god laughs
to see such sport

asks the human *what'll-it-be*
but knows: the usual

which unasked questions this time
and which blames

something about the icebox
whose turn to buy the plums again

the god-part sees the mirrors
how the human chooses this

to be small and seething
at the pouting boy-king

on high atop his
private narrative

so resourced
and so butthurt

COSMIC TANTRUM

My psychic says my anger
about this is outsized

but have you ever clenched
your soul into a fist? Some of us

plummet down every *Oh, well*
like a spell: *I can TOO*

do this thankless task. Saturn,
I misunderstood the ask—

can always pull a thousand
patterned kerchiefs from a pocket

of rage, quiet and competent.
Yes, ENJOY the sleeve bouquet;

I already SENT that fucking email.
It is true the great wolf Fenrir

held still as the gods bound him—
a Very Good Boy, flick of tail,

gleam of teeth everyone feared
until they didn't. *You made us*

do this to you, say the gods
of old, of capital, dysfunction.

What are boundaries to a tool?
How can the shadow speak

of personhood? Saturn, I wanted
to return me, felt my core collapse.

Chaos in orbit around nothing.
But this black hole isn't empty.

Someone vibrates near the center.
A dense, reactive knot.

Hello, I call to her.
I lower kerchiefs,

siphoning from the gods
my lowly magic.

QUEEN OF WANDS

In Florence, in our line somewhere, a strega. Witch.

Maybe she didn't exist, though ~*~*I want to believe*~*~

she could spirit away a wart on the hand with an old rag

and a whisper. Conduct power through electric palms. Or

maybe not. Somehow the cat tails always flick. We argue

over photos, lineage, which stories linger. Seventh daughter

of the seventh sister, seventh sister of the seventh daughter,

who remembers? Does it matter? As though everyone else

and birth order made her. Maybe they made her make her.

Firstborn daughter of the firstborn daughter of the firstborn

daughter. What does this placement mean under this sign?

On this auspicious day? In *this* economy? This house?

Someone's daughter. Someone's sister. Someone.

POSTURE OF DREAD

On the Four of Pentacles: somebody's body
clenched into a fist, posture of dread.

You have probably seen a dog posed so,
waiting for the always-other shoe.

The energy-worker says that *what upsets*
the neck is what we carry, eyebrow arched.

The chiropractor says, *We must open the chest*,
what aliens and healers call the heart-space.

Another fist: a redwood's thimble-cone,
which needs heat, even fire, to unclench

the seeds it grips, so small as to seem worthless—
why hide what doesn't even matter

which can neither be created nor destroyed.
A clip of an opening bud rewound, played backward.

Rewound as "did rewind," not "will re-wound"
but: what is wound around conceals a wound.

The reality star's *one weird trick* to avoid
wrinkles: *Just sleep on your back*, she says,

as though one could decide to feel safe.
Maybe one who's never felt like prey

can fall asleep with every organ up,
soft belly out, heart open to the stars

and predators. The witch says,
at the trailhead, *make the heart*

an altar. On it I place redwood cones
and matches, coins, a cup of water

for the Local Beast. And meet the eye
that rides a wave of sand, and the woman

who flickers, unclenching,
black fox and white cat.

NOTHING TRANCE

the dog is not chasing the cat—

nothing eats what you don't leave
    at the feet of trees
        in woods you visit in dreams

some say the inner child
    does not exist
        though you've made her in your mind

the way you must first make
    all things
        you later negate

so no dog, no cat, no problem
    as you sit there, traveling
        to a filled hole in your memory

feeling the temperature
    of that placeless place's air
        against your skin

and as the sensations and figures
    take shape, you begin to experience
        deep relaxation

remembering every word
    you never said, the exact feel
        of unspoken statements

reach for them
    remember how they pressed
        their weightless weight

nothing has matter
nothing matters

you will wake
feeling so heavy
full but empty

GUIDED MEDITATION WITH INNER MOTHER

No surprise that she's a witch
chopping ginger with garlic
sipped with honey, rosemary,
lemon, and vinegar, astringent

too-muchness against illness.
Her palms are warm, magnetic,
send electric currents through skin.
An awareness of a well

she never fills. She needs space
a certain way, conditions
optimal to forgetting being
anywhen or where. She could

pay more attention, stronger
tethers to a body she runs
like a horse skeleton. Place
your hand on one of hers. Yes,

the one holding a pen, papers
fanned around her. Tell her
what you need. Until the pupils
focus. She can grant what is asked.

Is soft, but not to be crossed.
will let none cross you either,
like a gate of roses—thorns
and salt and sage guarding you
always.

ADVICE FROM AN UPPER GRADER

ask not for whom the hamburger helps

dig deep enough in mud and you'll find clay

everyone please stop yelling at me, we yell, yellingly

the meaning of that six-line pointed S is yours alone

a stretch feels better when you scream it

don't trust anyone impressed with their own selflessness

twist from the stem to lap a honeysuckle's single drop of nectar

a need is the bottom of a valley of lack

the mouthfeel of a crunched crayon . . . is unparalleled

there's the land*lord* and the grounds*keeper*: the owner, and the one
who tends

real cheese doesn't gleam like patent leather

eat a piece of lichen off your costume, no one's looking

when they snarl like wild cats, they are afraid

the difference between being babied and being Baby is who's in charge

this is the project: to make yourself in your own image

EXHIBITION: *WHAT IS IT LIKE TO MAKE SOMETHING THAT MATTERS?*

Fig. 1
Woman Possessed by the Spirit of Despair
[Pictured: Photograph. Woman, late twenties, slumped in a desk chair before two computer monitors. Below her, a desk calendar's frenetic scribbling suggests a chalkboard theorem in a film about credibility. The bird trapped in her ribs has a death wish. When the phone rings, she steels herself against it. A calendar is calling. A receipt. An insult. A password. The mistress, then the wife. The dry cleaner's. A magazine. Her life?]
Anonymous. Digital photo print on archival paper, February 2019.

Fig. 2
The Scream
[Pictured: Painting. Ambiguous humanoid figure on a bridge, bald, hands sliding down the face, mouth a perfect howling O. Two shadow figures in the background recede or advance—it doesn't matter—they are always lurking at the corner of awareness, aren't they, beneath a sky gone haywire. Boats melt. The figure melts. It is not even lunch yet.]
Edvard Munch. Oil, tempera, pastel, and crayon on cardboard, 1893.

Fig. 3
Hi, Sarah
[Pictured: Printout of an Outlook email. Clear tape runs down the spine-like center, patching over violent rupture. The printed text makes reference to {redacted}. Says, "The *other* assistant found a way." Handwritten on the back, notes for the latest PR fluff piece on energetic tile, plush velvets, "honesty" of material—which is funny. Isn't it.]
[Redacted.]

Fig. 4
Mayor George B. McClellan, front row center, and other city officials inspect the subway in 1904*, courtesy of *The New York Times
[Pictured: Retouched newspaper photo. Rows of men in suits and boater hats sit on what looks like a wooden barge. McClellan is really there. One of the "other city officials" is an impostor; someone painted him a new face. They did a shitty job. Imagine drawing (painting?) such attention to some should-be-hidden error. Or thinking this looks "real *enough*." Imagine being asked to do something so stupid, and to lie. Imagine thinking no one would notice.]
Missing attribution. Digital print of photo and shenanigans on newsprint, April 11, 2019.

Fig. 5
Monkey Christ / Ecce Homo
[Pictured: Retouched painting resembling a rhesus monkey: straight nose, whole oval face haloed in hair. The mouth an O that whispers into haze. This portrait was Jesus once. Some civilian saw the flaking original fresco, thought, "Someone should *do* something." Thought, "Fuck, *I* could fix that." She could not. Such confidence. Doubled down on good intentions when questioned. Funny? Sad? Should she have done it? Probably not. A casualty. A treasure. The internet has spoken: we love it.]
Cecilia Giménez, attempted restoration, 2012 / Elías García Martínez, fresco, 1930.

Fig. 6
Portrait of the Artist as a Vain Child
[Pictured: Photograph. Four preschoolers watch a movie in their pajamas. Only one looks at the camera. You guessed it. On her face, the artist has dented the photograph with ballpoint pen, drawing three long eyelashes above each of her eyes. Sweet little beebs: the one in the picture who looks to the photographer, and the kindergartener who thought the eyelashes would look real, an improvement, dark and vertical and cartoon-thick. Should she have done it? Does it matter? A treasure. Tenderness for the little trickster, making something, anything, that pleased her.]
Sarah Lyn Rogers. Mixed media; pen on Kodak photo print, ca. 1995.

Fig. 7
Woman Watching* The Man Who Killed Don Quixote *at 2:00 a.m. on a Workday
[Pictured: Photograph. The spirit of despair, temporarily displaced. For two hours, the woman is filled only with this movie, about a man named Toby who hates his job as a director—he is tired of making bullshit for pay, he wants the authenticity he captured once in a student film, hiring amateur actors from towns in rural Spain, not knowing he cursed his lead to *become* Don Quixote. Sometimes authenticity is dangerous. Sometimes authenticity is fake. The "real" Don Quixote was invented by the book character Alonso Quixano, himself invented by author Miguel de Cervantes. So: a character inside of Toby's film, which is inside of Terry Gilliam's film, is channeling the character Alonso, who is pretending and then believing himself to be a character called Don Quixote, written by Cervantes. What was it about this movie? Adam Driver's swiveling hips? The absurdity, theatrics? Being quite literally possessed by literature? A four-hundred-year chain of art-making? Men using their powers for art? Invoking old words that still matter? That *anything* fucking matters? It took real-director Terry Gilliam nearly thirty years to make *The Man Who Killed Don Quixote*, as though it were cursed. It was released in the US for only one night. The movie-screen light falls on the woman's face. Something unacknowledged glows.]
Anonymous. Digital photo print on archival paper, April 10, 2019.

Fig 8.
Woman Possessed by the Spirit of Escape
[Pictured: The woman smiles—last day in purgatory. She wears a summer dress and heels, lips red. Between the ringing phones and calendars and melting shadows and the screaming, she has taken other calls. Set up "dentist appointments," lying the way they have taught her. Her skin glows for the first time in a year. Everyone asks why she is "all dressed up." She tells the truth: she is in a holiday mood. After, she'll leave for a weekend of art-making, time off, a new job where she'll make some things that please her. Now she can float at will, rising out of the frame, beyond the desk and walls and scaffolding, beyond anyone's reach. She is rising where no one can see her, can get {to} her. She is rising where she decides who can, and if.]
Sarah Lyn Rogers. Mental picture, June 2019. Gift of the artist.

IN WHICH MUSIC ACTIVATES THE VENTRAL VAGAL

To the body, walking folder named "sort later"—
I hold you now so tender, little bee, more than
a worker stomaching whatever into honey.
To the ones who held you when all I could fathom
was our Badness—song, breath, chest, our friends
alive forever in the sound, unknowing wisdom
of a long note's long exhale. To the holy dark
of soft-voiced angels. To the frequencies
that moved the density. *You have always*
processed the emotions of the entire family.
Soft one, slumped over the steering wheel,
face swiped stop-motion by sodium lights—
they couldn't wring you out if you were dry.
Climb the notes to dissonance, that honesty.
A fellow who has also been destroyed:
what we recognize in artworks that destroy me.

GUIDED MEDITATION WITH DEAD MUSICIAN

Okay, close your eyes, deep breath.
As if it wasn't enough, the years
spent rotating the same five CDs
feeling some resonance beyond

the actual notes, those nimble-
fingered descants over bass line
melodies thrumming through
your teenage body, soundtrack

of your first car, the red one
low to the ground and three
years older than your own
resigned self, girl driving alone

at night to and from the boys
who didn't know you, or friends
who wanted to but didn't either,
not that you could show them

anyone. Felt like no one
but the singer with *spiderweb-
thin delivery* could understand
a constant low-level sadness

rising ecstatically to the top
of your consciousness with certain
chord changes. *This is what my soul
sounds like*, you were embarrassed to think,

but thought anyway, willed it
to the one who felt kindred but died
six months before you'd heard of him.
All anyone can ever think to say

is *R.I.P.*, the same comments
under videos and song lyrics.
R.I.P., R.I.P., as though death
and not his gift *is* what he is.

Maybe they can't see themselves
in the songs' scenes, sitting alone
in a dim bar, walking alone
to a fight, waiting alone for a train

alone alone often alone but resonant
beyond physical space, beyond his
human body—

the way you now
breathe, listen, exist

inside yourself and also
in the place that has no name.

ARS POETICA WITH NEED AND WILD CATS

Childhood, I knew you as a long hypnotic dream,
fed on a steady diet of adrenaline. Adulthood

dreams in series, unlocked chambers
filled with rising water. I thought

there'd be less magic up here
in the growing bright that makes me squint

but for my first trick I will make the air
feel different from my skin—do you read me,

have you ever felt your outline, would you like to?
Here I say "you" and mean "reader" and also

"little-me," but I know that we are separate.
Reader, I would not presume to share

your temperature. *Are you cold?* somebody
used to ask, a statement and request. They were,

and I should offer remedy. A whole locked chamber
of intent smuggled through and under "you."

For my next trick, I seam-rip the layered words.
For my last, I summon back the old wisdom,

each so-called inanimate object alive in its way.
Young, I was alive in my way. Now I am alive

in ways observable even to the 3D eye. No longer
snarl-shamed against claiming anger.

As a toddler, I loved a stuffed tiger. Squeezed it
with such pressure the head fell off, Frankenstein-

stitched back together. "Fell" is a gentle word,
dishonest. Forced, maybe, by accident—white-knuckle

hugged it in my sleep. *You loved that thing so much*
the head fell off, somebody said, as though "love"

encompasses violence. I too have been a head
without a body, body without a head. We do

what we can to get by until we can breathe,
cut a wide mouth in the hood of burrs we wore

for reasons lost to time. I too have been a totem,
like Natalie Wood's sacred entourage of stuffed tigers,

haloed everywhere around her, how she thought
they could protect her from the screeching void.

Psychic defense isn't real, one might say of the tigers.
The clutching is. A totem knows it best, fears the sense

memory. Goes inside the white room of the mind,
pulls blood away from the extremities. I exit the white room

a whole woman, but I exit it for years, the long hall
of a never-ending dream. I smuggle, too. I smuggle

little-me. There is a tenderness that hasn't been
stitched over, one that asks to be held. She sneaks

into my speech, says *the internet no worky*, says
my sippy cup tastes like a pool toy. Says *I don't*

know what any of those words mean. Asks me
for the cheetahs at the checkstand, hamster-small

and wonky, at least the first one I pick up, put down,
pick up again, with one very symmetrical friend.

The crooked one lists to one side, like little-me's
smile in old photos. There is a child in me who knows

they are alive, in their way. I don't ask of them
protection. Who would believe it's in their power

to provide? When I hold them, it's with loose hands,
palms flat like a fledgling's branch-ledge,

or like the haloed woman's on the Strength card,
arms gentled under the lion's open jaws. I used

to think my strength was to prevent my being bitten.
But what if you just had skin, some always ask. I used

to want to be the thing that bites. Stuffed tiger,
I am sorry for the way I gripped you, by the neck.

Did you sigh when the seam last ripped?
Through that opened wound, could you breathe?

ACKNOWLEDGMENTS

Thank you to the following publications and presses where these poems previously appeared, some in different forms:

Dream Pop Journal: "The Content Is Supposed to Burst from the Container," "Exhibition: *What Is It Like to Make Something That Matters?*," "Golden Child Tantrum," "Please Answer to the Best of Your Ability," and "Self-Anthropology"

Forth: "The Empress" and "Tantrum about My Uterus"

Grimoire: "Guided Meditation with Inner Mother"

HAD: "APPLICANT MUST HAVE" and "LOCAL BEAST KIND OF A LITTLE BITCH, ACTUALLY"

Hobart: "I Could Signal Dominance in Email Correspondence as Trained but the Concept Is Offensive and I'm Baby" (Special thanks to guest editor Taylor Byas!)

Trampset: "Pot-Bound"

Witch Craft Mag: "To My Teenage Self, Who Always Fell for It" and "Some Brainwashed Dude on Twitter Insists That to Be Valuable a Woman Must Possess the Mathematically Perfect, Suspiciously Babylike Skull of an Angel"

Yes, Poetry: "Guided Meditation with Dead Musician," "Guided Meditation with Inner Child," and "Guided Meditation with Mean Voice"

ZYZZYVA: "Baby Island"

Many thanks to Ghost City Press, who published the following poems as a digital micro-chap entitled *Autocorrect Suggests "Tithe"*: "Autocorrect Suggests 'Tithe,'" "Guided Meditation with Mean Voice," "Let's Practice Kissing, Compare Bra Sizes," "Artfully Vague Trance," "Subtweeted Again in the Shared Google Doc," "Egg Trance," "Guided Meditation with Inner Child," "Guided Meditation with Inner Mother," "Guided Meditation with Dead Musician," and "Nothing Trance."

Thank you to Sgomento Zurigo gallery for commissioning the poem "You Are Instructed Not to Ask What It Is" on the occasion of the exhibition *Singalong* (March 17–April 23, 2023), featuring the art of Ken Kagami and Anders Dickson.

Thank you to these incredible writers who so generously gave their time and their wordsmithery to blurb the collection: Taylor Byas, Rachel Feder, Lucy Ives, and Mattilda Bernstein Sycamore. I appreciate you so much.

Thank you to Alex Rogers, Aly Schaefer, Bailey Cook Dailey, Miriam Vance, Jane Marchant, Alicia Kroell, Jordan Koluch, Sarah Brody, Abigail Gabriel, Olenka Burgess, and Lauren Friedlander for the deep talks while I worked with and through this. Thank you to Liza Fenster and Robin Doxey for your magic. Thank you to Jessa Reed, Yaya Erin Rivera Merriman, Natalie Ross, and Lindsay Mack for expanding my consciousness, and to Carolyn Lovewell for the concept of existential kink. Thank you to Jeff Hinshaw for teaching me the tarot and talking poetry and the cosmos with me. Thank you to the Chrissy Tolley Discord for being exactly the right space for cosmic tantrums.

Eternal thanks to Tinkerbell, for being the best damn cat the universe could bestow upon a human being. For teaching me so much about love, taking up space, and holding gently. Let's find each other again in the next one, okay?

Thank you to my editor, Marisa Siegel, for seeing and understanding and holding this book with gentle, open hands, and to the rest of the team at Northwestern University Press, including Christopher Bigelow, Parneshia Jones, Charlotte Keathley, Mary Klein, Iván Pérez-Zayas, Maddie Schultz, Courtney Smotherman, and Kristen Twardowski. And thank you to Marianne Jankowski for designing such a gorgeous book cover. Many thanks also to Alisha Gorder, Cassie Mannes Murray, and Pine State Publicity.

Thank you to some real ones who encouraged me through earlier versions of the manuscript—Leigh Stein, Yuka Igarashi, Candice Wuehle, Chrissy Tolley, Nahida Nisa—and who gave thoughtful feedback on individual poems: Jason Koo, Natalie Eilbert, Angel Nafis, Shira Erlichman, Gabrielle Bates, and Sweet Action Poetry. Thank you to Michael Chang for inviting me to share some of these poems at the *Synthetic Jungle* book launch, and to Brooklyn Poets for giving me a space to try these and other fledglings in front of a crowd.

Thank you to Emily Blair, who drove me to Grey Gardens.

Thank you to Kevin, who looks at me like maybe I am magic.

NOTES

The opening sentences of "Artfully Vague Trance," "Egg Trance," and "Nothing Trance" all come from *Trance-Formations: Neuro-Linguistic Programming and the Structure of Hypnosis* by John Grinder and Richard Bandler, edited by Connirae Andreas (Real People Press, 1981).

Italicized or quoted Edie lines in the following *Grey Gardens* poems are actual dialogue from the 1975 documentary by Albert and David Maysles: "Despite Many Proclamations, Little Edie Never Leaves Big Edie at Grey Gardens," " 'That's All I Need—an Ordered Life,' " and "Universally Relatable Writing Prompts, Part II." The quote "The only vermin here is you" is from the prequel documentary, *That Summer* (2017), directed by Göran Hugo Olsson.

The quote in "Universally Relatable Writing Prompts, Part II" that begins "Innocence is a relic of a time . . ." is from artist and writer Molly Crabapple's essay for *Vice*, "On Turning 30."

Please, please do a web search for "Mayor George B. McClellan, front row center, and other city officials inspect the subway in 1904." The retouched photo is so good, so bad.